# MAGIC
## ★ ★ JOHNSON ★ ★

### BASKETBALL'S
### SMILING
### SUPERSTAR

# MAGIC
## ★ ★ JOHNSON ★ ★

## BASKETBALL'S SMILING SUPERSTAR

## By Rick L. Johnson

Taking part BOOKS

DILLON PRESS
New York

Maxwell Macmillan Canada
Toronto

Maxwell Macmillan International
New York   Oxford   Singapore   Sydney

**Photo Credits**

All photos courtesy of AP—Wide World Photos.

**Library of Congress Cataloging-in-Publication Data**

Johnson, Rick L.
    Magic Johnson : basketball's smiling superstar / by Rick L. Johnson.
        p.    cm. — (A Taking part biography)
    Includes bibliographical references (p.    ).
        Summary: A biography of the star guard for the Los Angeles Lakers who shocked
fans by retiring in 1991 because he had contracted the AIDS virus.
        ISBN 0-87518-553-3
        1. Johnson, Earvin, 1959-    —Juvenile literature. 2. Basketball players—United
States—Biography—Juvenile literature.
    [1. Johnson, Earvin, 1959–    . 2. Basketball players. 3. Afro-Americans—Biography.]
    I. Title. II. Series.
    GV884.J63J64  1992                                                              92-3175
    796.323'092—dc20
    [B]

Dillon Press                                     Maxwell Macmillan Canada, Inc.
Macmillan Publishing Company                     1200 Eglinton Avenue East
866 Third Avenue                                 Suite 200
New York, NY  10022                              Don Mills, Ontario M3C 3N1

Macmillan Publishing Company is part of the Maxwell Communication Group of
Companies.

First edition

Printed in the United States of America

10    9    8    7    6    5    4    3    2    1

# ★ CONTENTS

*Magic Johnson's skill and enthusiasm made him one of the best players in the NBA.*

## PREFACE

# EARVIN "MAGIC" JOHNSON

Perhaps no basketball player has ever displayed as many talents as Earvin "Magic" Johnson has.

With his 6'9" height, he could grab an opponent's missed shot. Then, turning, he could skillfully dribble downcourt, head up with eyes wide as he scanned the floor. Suddenly, without even looking in that direction, he might flip the ball to a teammate for a basket. Or he might smoothly score the basket himself.

Equally important to Magic's success was his zest for the game. Throughout his many years of playing ball, he inspired his teammates to play their best. The result, from high school through his professional career, was championship after championship.

His style also excited crowds. When he flashed his famous smile, fans could share in the joy he felt. They now share in the hurt, too, since November 1991, when he announced he is carrying HIV, the virus that causes AIDS.

Because of his talent and personality, Magic's fans can be found throughout the world.

# Chapter 1

# A STRANGER THERE BUT ONCE

Los Angeles Laker guard Byron Scott knew something was wrong. He could tell by the tone of Coach Mike Dunleavy's voice.

"Two o'clock, I want you at the Forum," he ordered the team. "If you have something planned to do, cancel it."

Driving home from the early Thursday practice, Scott tried to think what might be wrong. His running mate at guard, Earvin "Magic" Johnson, had missed practices and games for about two weeks. He prayed the meeting wasn't about Earvin, about his friend having a serious illness. Maybe, he hoped, it was about somebody being traded from the team.

That afternoon Scott watched as Johnson, wearing his usual smile, walked into the Laker locker room at the Forum. Then came the bad news. Magic told the team that he would be retiring. He had the virus that could lead to AIDS.

Some of the Lakers began to cry, but not Magic. He said

*Magic Johnson makes the announcement that he is infected with HIV, the virus that leads to AIDS.*

he had to stay strong, and he asked them to stay strong for him.

At three o'clock that day, November 7, 1991, Johnson entered a Forum room packed with reporters and television cameras. As he spoke to the world, he tried to be upbeat. "It's another challenge, another chapter in my life. My back is against the wall. I think you just have to come out swinging, and I'm swinging."

The virus that causes AIDS, called the human immunodeficiency virus, or HIV, can take from a few months or many years to develop into full-blown AIDS. Until then, a person's health can appear unchanged. Johnson was retiring, according to Laker doctor Michael Mellman, because of the extreme physical demands of pro basketball.

Magic said he would try to educate people about AIDS, which stands for acquired immune deficiency syndrome. HIV is most often spread through intimate sexual contact or the sharing of unsterilized drug works by drug users. Johnson said he'd gotten the virus from intimate sexual contact with an infected partner.

There are drugs used to treat HIV and AIDS, but there is as yet no cure. Although a person may live for a number of years with the disease, doctors consider HIV infection ultimately fatal.

Many people admired the courage Johnson showed at the press conference as he talked about his uncertain future. That, though, was little comfort to Byron Scott.

"The way he handled it shows the type of person he is," Scott told the *Los Angeles Times*. "But it didn't make it any easier for the people who love him."

Less than seven months earlier, Magic's teammates and fans had cheered as he became professional basketball's all-time assist leader. In basketball, credit for an assist is given for a pass that leads to a basket. When Johnson broke the National Basketball Association (NBA) record on April 15, Forum officials stopped the game. During a 15-minute ceremony, Magic tearfully thanked his parents for all they had done for him.

"Without those two beautiful people, the 'Magic Makers,' I wouldn't be here," Johnson told the crowd.

Earvin Johnson, Jr., was born to Christine and Earvin Johnson, Sr., on August 14, 1959, in Lansing, Michigan. Earvin was the fourth of their seven children. His father also had three children from an earlier marriage.

To support this large family, Earvin, Sr., had two jobs.

*A tearful Magic Johnson thanks his parents for their support after breaking the NBA record for assists.*

During the late afternoons and evenings, he worked at a factory that made the metal bodies for cars. To earn more money, he bought a truck and started his own shop-cleaning and trash-hauling route.

With his father so busy, Earvin saw little of him during the week. There were many special times with him on weekends, though. They often went to a local track to see dragsters race. But Earvin's favorite time with his father was on Sunday afternoons, when they watched NBA games on television.

His father, who was 6'4", had played basketball in high school. He openly shared with Earvin both his love for the game and his knowledge of its skills. "Dad made me see the importance of the little things in basketball," Johnson recalls in his book *Magic's Touch*, written with Roy S. Johnson. The basics were important even to the pros, his father pointed out.

Soon Earvin set out to master one of those basic skills: dribbling. Sitting on the porch of their two-story home, he dribbled. Returning from the store for his mother, he carried groceries in one arm, and with the other, he dribbled. Going to the grade school courts two blocks away, of course he dribbled.

Starting in the fourth grade, Earvin often played full-court

*Always a close family, Earvin Sr. and Christine Johnson join Magic and his wife to celebrate a win.*

one-on-one against his brother Larry, who was one year older. Larry liked to pretend he was Walt Frazier, then a New York Knicks defensive star. He pressed Earvin all over the court. Although that sometimes made Earvin angry, it helped him become even better at dribbling.

Earvin spent much of his free time playing basketball, but he also liked music. Some summer nights, he and his friends would gather at a street corner to sing. He was in the children's choir at church, and he learned to play the bass guitar.

There were also chores to do, such as mowing the lawn or emptying the trash. When he was in the fifth grade, Earvin's mother began work as a school janitor. With their parents away, Quincy, Larry, Earvin, Lily Pearl, Kim, Evelyn, and Yvonne sometimes had minor fights. The brothers and sisters knew how hard their parents worked, though, and they usually tried to behave.

One of the punishments that hurt Earvin the most was given by his fifth-grade teacher, Greta Dart. After Earvin failed to turn in an assignment, she told him he could not play in the next basketball game.

"But it's for the championship," Earvin argued. He was the

star of the Main Street School team. The coach was Jim Dart, his teacher's husband. Neither Coach Dart nor Earvin's mother would ask Mrs. Dart to change her mind.

"Earvin always wanted to win," said Mr. Dart, who also coached Earvin in sixth grade. "He was an excellent, excellent player. Most teams we played could not compete against us."

The only game Earvin's teams lost during those two years was the one in which he wasn't allowed to play. He held no hard feelings toward his fifth-grade teacher, though. In fact, he grew close to both Jim and Greta Dart. They took him to watch many high-school basketball games. And Earvin, growing rapidly, often stopped by the Dart home for an extra meal.

During two summers, he helped Mr. Dart deliver soft drinks to stores. As Earvin placed bottles on shelves, Dart soon noticed his skill in dealing with others—even adults. "He would look around to see that he was doing things the right way, and he was always polite."

Store owners and clerks along the route, Dart recalled, began to look forward to seeing his friendly young helper. "He had this ability to charm people. Wherever he went, he was a stranger there but once." Even without a basketball, everyone

*Magic's winning smile and good humor made him a favorite with every team he played on.*

remembered Earvin.

In junior high, more and more people in Lansing heard about Earvin's basketball skills. He kept growing, and his teams kept winning. He reached 6' in seventh grade and 6'4" in eighth grade. Both years his teams won the city championship for their grade level.

Then in ninth grade, his last year at Dwight Rich Junior High, Earvin's team lost the title. Even though the loss was to a school led by Jay Vincent, a future NBA player, Earvin was crushed. He felt down for weeks.

Something else was also bothering Earvin. He worried about starting high school. In grade school, he had dreamed of playing for Sexton High School. It was only half a mile from his home, and he had gone to many games there. Sexton, attended mainly by black students, was where most of his friends would go.

But a recent law, designed to create more racial balance in the schools, had ended his dream of playing for Sexton. He would be bused to Everett High School, which was attended mostly by white students.

His oldest brother, Quincy, had been among the first

black students bused to Everett. At that time, whites had staged protests against busing, and there had been brick throwing and fights in the school. That violence had ended, but his other brother, Larry, said that blacks were still not treated fairly at the school.

Earvin had never had any trouble getting along with people. But that didn't mean he was looking forward to going to Everett.

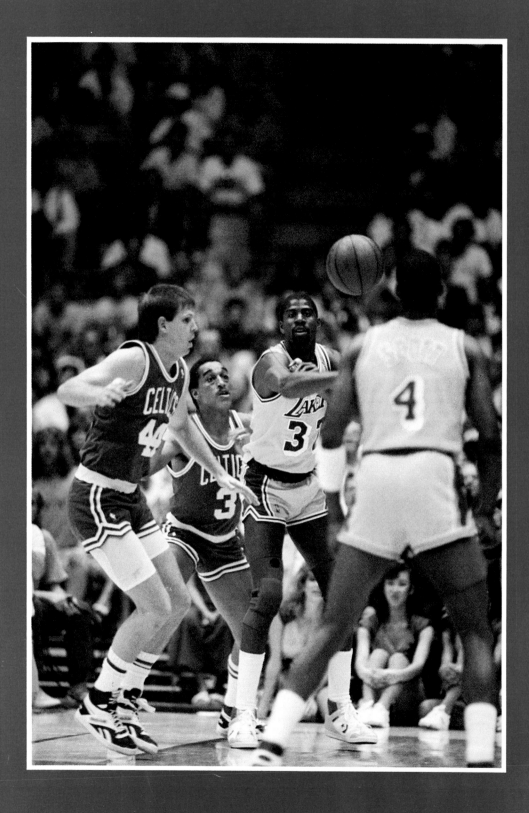

# Chapter 2

# EARVIN JOHNSON'S SCHOOL

Sportswriter Fred Stabley, Jr., had seen several high-school basketball games featuring players who later starred in the NBA. Never, though, had he seen anyone perform like Earvin Johnson.

Only a sophomore at Everett High School, Johnson had done everything possible to destroy the talented Jackson Parkside team. He finished with 36 points, 18 rebounds, 16 assists, and 5 steals.

In the locker room, Stabley watched reporters and young fans swarm around Everett's star. Johnson treated the adults with respect, and he treated the children as if they were all his little buddies. This kid is really special, Stabley thought. Someone should give him a nickname.

Finally, when the crowd left, Stabley stepped up to Johnson. "Earvin, we've got to call you something. 'Big E' is out because of Elvin Hayes, and 'Dr. J' is out because of Julius Erving." This young athlete had played such a tremendous

*Magic learned many of the moves that would make him a star with the Lakers while he was still a player in high school.*

game. And the way he smiled and made those around him smile was amazing. It was as though he had some kind of magical powers.

"How about 'Magic'?" Stabley asked.

Earvin, still sitting by his locker, looked up at him and flashed a big smile. "That's okay with me, Mr. Stabley," he politely agreed.

The more Earvin saw the nickname Magic in the *Lansing State Journal*, the more he liked it. His parents, though, didn't. They were afraid it would lead people to expect too much from him. But during his sophomore year, he lived up to the nickname. He averaged 22.3 points a game and made first team all-city and second team all-state. Everett finished with a 22–2 record.

The next year, Magic's coach, George Fox, moved him to point guard. A player in that position often dribbles the ball up the floor and directs the team's offense. Someone Johnson's size (6'6" as a junior) usually plays nearer the basket, at forward or center. But Fox wanted to make full use of Magic's ball-handling and passing skills. Johnson responded by averaging 25.8 points a game, making first team all-state and leading Everett to a 24–2 record.

Good things also happened off the court. During his sophomore year, he became close friends with teammate Reggie Chastine, a year older and also black. In the classroom, Earvin maintained nearly a B average. Working for the school newspaper, he advanced to head of advertising.

As he made new friends and the basketball team played well, his earlier feelings about attending Everett faded. Teachers and coaches saw fewer racial problems at the school, and many credited Magic.

"Earvin Johnson crossed the color barrier and was loved and accepted by whites as well as blacks," Coach Fox said. "Earvin was color-blind, but he was not only that way with race, he was that way about everything. Whether he met a ten-year-old child or the mayor, he would take time to listen to both."

Magic's fame quickly spread throughout the state. Once, at a meeting of school principals, Everett principal Frank Throop introduced himself, saying he was from Everett High School.

"That's Earvin Johnson's school," someone responded, in a tone that made it sound as if Magic owned the school.

After thinking a moment, Throop had to agree. "That's

*Always looking for fun, Magic takes time out to play with some young fans.*

about right, it's Earvin's school," he replied in the same tone.

While Magic made a powerful impact at Everett, one person made an extra-strong influence on Earvin's own life. Charles Tucker, a Lansing school psychologist, had played college basketball and had had several pro tryouts. Tucker often played one-on-one with Earvin, and he took him to many NBA games.

"[He] helped me focus my goals," Johnson recalls in one of his early books, *Magic*, written with Richard Levin. "Tuck" showed him the mental and physical toughness it would take to become a pro player.

Another major influence on Magic during his high-school years was Coach Fox. Earvin had always worked hard, both on and off the court. In junior high, he was a janitor in an office building. In high school, he was a stockboy at Quality Dairy. Now, on the basketball floor, Coach Fox pushed him harder than ever before.

If teammates couldn't challenge Magic in a drill, then Coach Fox pulled out his stopwatch. "Beat the clock," Fox ordered. The coach demanded all-out effort every day. Magic learned that only by working his hardest in practice could he play his hardest in a game.

Magic had another reason to work hard his senior year. The summer before, his best friend, Reggie Chastine, had been killed in an auto accident. The team dedicated its 1976-1977 season to Reggie.

Magic, named a preseason high-school all-American, went on a scoring spree. Early in his senior year, he was averaging more than 40 points a game. Although the Everett Vikings won each contest, Coach Fox was not happy. He called his star player into his office.

"Earvin, if you continue to score your 45 points a game, we'll never win the state championship," Fox warned. "Somewhere down the line, there will be a critical time when we'll need one of your teammates to produce. They won't be ready unless you cut your average in half and get everybody involved."

For a moment, Earvin looked surprised. But as he left the office, Fox knew he had understood.

"I gotcha, Coach," Earvin said.

He certainly had. The next game, Magic scored only 12 points, but he passed out 18 assists. The team's average margin of victory rose to 40 points a game.

The Vikings remained undefeated until Jay Vincent's team, Eastern High, upset them late in the regular season. But Everett came back to win a rematch with Eastern in the district play-offs. The Vikings then marched to the state finals, where they met Brother Rice High School.

Everett seemed to have won the game, but a Brother Rice shot from beyond half-court sent the contest into overtime. Was Everett's bad luck in the state tournament going to continue? During Magic's sophomore year, the Vikings had lost in the quarterfinals. During his junior year, they had lost in the semifinals.

In the 1977 finals against Brother Rice, the Vikings raced to a 56–50 overtime lead. But Magic fouled out with 1:06

remaining. Everett would have to hold the lead without its star. During his senior season, Magic had averaged 28.8 points, 16.0 rebounds, and 7.4 assists. Now, just as Coach Fox had predicted, someone besides Magic would have to score critical points.

And they did. While Magic cheered from the sidelines, Everett held on for a 62–56 win. Earvin and Coach Fox did a victory dance at midcourt. The Vikings were 27–1 and state champions! An Everett fan helped Earvin lift Coach Fox into the air.

All around Magic, his school celebrated.

Chapter 3

# BORN TO BE A SPARTAN

Returning from a high-school all-star team tour, Magic Johnson stepped off the plane and surveyed the crowd. On the left were University of Michigan fans, and on the right were Michigan State University boosters. Each group held signs urging him to attend its favorite school.

Magic felt pulled in two directions as he tried to decide where to go to college. His mother believed he would receive the best education at Michigan, in Ann Arbor. His father wanted him to stay near home and attend Michigan State, in East Lansing.

Magic himself was torn. Michigan had the strongest basketball tradition, and several good players were returning. There he might play on a National Collegiate Athletic Association (NCAA) championship team. However, Michigan State was the school he had rooted for while he was growing up. And when he gave basketball clinics for the boys' club, his young fans begged him to play for the hometown team.

*Reaching for a basket, Magic shows off the determination*
*that made him a star player in college.*

He knew that whichever school he chose, some people would be disappointed. When he finally decided, the person he hated to tell was his mother. People often commented on his smile, and he felt he had gotten it from her. She almost always smiled. But it faded when he said he had chosen Michigan State.

"I've always been for the underdog," he told her.

On April 22, 1977, at a press conference at Everett High School, he announced his decision. "When it came right down to it," he said, "I don't think I could have gone anywhere else. I was born to be a Spartan."

Magic's talents helped Michigan State even more than most had expected. The previous season, the Spartans had suffered through a 10–17 record. In Magic's freshman year, they finished 25–5 and won the Big Ten Conference for the first time in 19 years.

Of course, there were some adjustments to make that first season. Most of them, though, were on the part of Magic's teammates.

"The toughest thing they had to get used to was how good he was," sportswriter Fred Stabley, Jr., recalled. "They'd be

*Magic tells the fans that he is number one.*

running down the floor and the next thing you know—bam!—the ball hits them in the side. They didn't even know they were open, but Earvin did. And they'd look like the idiot, because if they had been paying attention, they would have had a lay-up."

Johnson averaged 17.0 points his freshman year. However, as a 6'8" point guard, his ball-handling and passing skills meant the most to Michigan State. "In Earvin's case, you don't talk about the points he scores, but the points he produces," said Spartan coach Jud Heathcote.

As only a freshman, Johnson was named all-Big Ten and

31

all-American. "He enjoyed being the center of attention, but he never seemed to get a big head," Stabley remembered. "He really liked kids, as opposed to the adoring adult fans. He didn't mind the adults, but I think he got more of a kick out of the kids."

After each home game, young fans waited near the locker room to ask for his autograph. Magic always took time for them, even if he had seen some of the same faces for several games in a row. "To me there isn't a sweeter sound in the world than a child's laughter," he once remarked.

Johnson also made time for studying. He maintained between a B and C grade average as a communications major. Magic was interested in the business side of radio and television more than such areas as announcing.

During his first year, Johnson lived in a dormitory, with former rival Jay Vincent as his roommate. In his free time, he enjoyed going to the mall to buy records or playing pool at the student union. He also liked to dance at dormitory parties or Lansing discos.

"There is time for business, time for school, and time for fun," Magic told *Sports Illustrated*. "Things can be happening

*Magic goes for a hook shot.*

at a party before I get there, but when I show up, they just happen more."

Sometimes at discos, Magic served as the disc jockey, choosing records and making comments to the crowd. "This is E. J. your deejay talking to you," he would begin in the rich, vibrating tone of an announcer.

He also used that voice on the Spartan bus or plane to "liven things up," according to teammate Gerald Gilkie. "He'd make up little stories about the coaches and players that everyone would laugh at."

A serious time for the Spartans, though, came midway through Magic's sophomore year. After playing well early in the season, they started the conference schedule with only a 4–4 record. Then came an important home contest against Ohio State, 8–0 in Big Ten play.

"Michigan State took the lead, but then Earvin went down with a sprained ankle," Stabley recalled. "In the training room, he was listening to the game on the radio. When he heard Ohio State fight back to take the lead, he jumped up and said, 'I've got to go back in.'"

As he returned to the court, the crowd's roar shook Jenison

Field House. Magic's play fired the Spartans to an 84–79 overtime victory that turned their season around. They went on to tie for the conference title, then raced to the NCAA championship tournament in Salt Lake City.

There Michigan State won its semifinal game, with Magic scoring 29 points in a 101–67 rout of Pennsylvania. Undefeated Indiana State won the other semifinal game, with Larry Bird pouring in 35 points against De Paul. Johnson and Bird, the two most exciting young players in basketball, would meet on March 26, 1979, for the NCAA title.

Michigan State opened the game with a swarming zone defense that slowed Bird's scoring. The Spartans took a 37–28 halftime lead. However, both Magic and Michigan State's other all-American, Greg Kelser, were in foul trouble. Midway through the second half, Indiana State pulled to within 6 points. The Spartans regained control, though, and won the game, 75–64.

Johnson finished with 24 points, 7 rebounds, and 10 assists. Bird finished with 19 points, 13 rebounds, and 2 assists. Magic had outperformed Bird, and Michigan State had earned the national title!

*Magic tries to block a shot made by Patrick Ewing of the New York Knicks.*

The celebration reached a peak the next day as the team stood at the center of a packed Jenison Field House. Once again, screaming and stomping shook the building. Magic moved to the microphone, but it was too noisy for him to speak. Waiting for the Spartan fans to grow quiet, he smiled and laughed, which only made them cheer even louder.

As usual, the crowd was under Magic's spell.

Chapter 4

# THE BIG FELLA'S HERE

The Los Angeles Lakers gathered at the airport to fly to Philadelphia. Waiting to board the plane, they heard the bad news about their star center, 7'2" Kareem Abdul-Jabbar. The "Big Fella," as Magic liked to call him, would not play in game six of the NBA championship series. He had a badly sprained ankle.

"E. J., you're starting at center tomorrow night," Laker coach Paul Westhead said.

Magic thought the coach was joking, and he decided to play along. When he boarded the plane, he slid into the left front seat. This was where Kareem usually sat. "Don't worry," he repeated over and over, grinning at each teammate as they walked by. "The Big Fella's here."

Everyone laughed. The idea that the 20-year-old rookie could take Kareem's place was so farfetched it was funny. Abdul-Jabbar would be named the NBA's Most Valuable Player that season, the sixth time he'd be so honored. In the 1980

*Magic takes charge of the ball.*

finals against the Philadelphia 76ers, he'd been averaging 33 points and 13 rebounds a game. His outstanding play had led Los Angeles to a 3–2 game lead.

The Lakers still needed one more win for the title. Experts said their only hope was that Abdul-Jabbar would recover in time to play in game seven. No one thought Los Angeles could win game six in front of more than 18,000 hostile Philadelphia fans.

Magic and the Lakers, though, believed they could. Coach Westhead was serious about his rookie playing center. To win, the team needed to focus on the fast break and rebounding. Magic would have to help in both areas.

During the first half, the Lakers surprised everyone by playing even with Philadelphia, 60–60. Then they scored the first 14 points of the second half. Magic was on his way to a fantastic game. "It was as though I was in another world," he said. "I felt like I could do anything."

He finished with 42 points, 15 rebounds, and 7 assists. In sparking the Lakers' 123–107 win, he played one of the best all-around games in the history of basketball. Not only his skill, but his spirited style attracted fans.

*Kareem Abdul-Jabbar and Magic—the Lakers' Dynamic Duo*

"Even as a fierce competitor, I try to find time for a smile," he says in *Magic's Touch.*

Johnson had turned professional after his sophomore year at Michigan State. The city of Los Angeles quickly fell in love with its newest star. The Lakers' attendance at the Forum increased by almost 2,500 per game from the previous season. Once Johnson greeted former football star O. J. Simpson in the locker room. "What's happenin'?" Magic asked him. O. J. knew the answer. "*You're* what's happenin'," he declared.

On his nights off, Johnson often went dancing in Los Angeles discos. During his first few years with the Lakers, he lived in an apartment. His son, Andre, was born during this time, but Magic and Andre's mother never married. In 1984 Magic moved into a $2.5 million mansion in Bel Air, an area near Los Angeles. His home featured a party room with space for dancing and a spot equipped for "E. J. the Deejay." It also included an indoor basketball court and an outdoor heated pool.

During the off-season, Magic enjoyed playing softball. Throughout the year, there was time for card games with friends. In addition to his teammates, he became friends with the Detroit Pistons' all-star guard Isiah Thomas. Growing up in strong families had been important to both Isiah and Magic. With much in common, Magic felt that he could share his inner feelings with Isiah.

Magic and several of his friends, including Isiah, purchased a radio station in Evergreen, Colorado. Johnson also made investments in real estate, oil, and gas. Early in his career, he signed contracts to promote Converse and Spalding products.

His basketball camps quickly became one of his favorite interests outside of pro basketball. Some young players were surprised at how hard Magic made them work at the camps. "I drive them because I believe in working hard," Magic explained.

Many thought he simply relied on his talent to create fancy passes during the heat of an NBA contest. "Chances are that anything you see me do during a game I've done a thousand times in practice," he told the young players.

Of course, his hard work did not always mean a championship for his team. During his second year as a professional, Magic injured his left knee and missed 45 games. In the play-offs against Houston, his last-second shot that would have given the Lakers the series win fell short.

Los Angeles regained the championship in 1982, but there

*Magic displays the moves that made him a hit with Lakers fans.*

were problems for Magic. Early in the season he clashed with Coach Westhead about how the coach should run the team's offense. Magic, along with Laker owner Jerry Buss, was unhappy with attempts to slow the team's fast-break style. When Buss fired Westhead, many fans blamed Johnson for the coach's losing his job. For several weeks, he was booed. That hurt Magic, but the boos became cheers as the Lakers rolled to another title under new coach Pat Riley.

In 1983 the Lakers reached the NBA finals before losing to Julius Erving's 76ers. Then in the 1984 championship series, Magic and Los Angeles faced another superstar: Larry Bird of the Boston Celtics.

Most people considered Magic and Bird the two best all-around players in basketball. But which one was *the* best was the subject of heated debate. The nation's basketball fans looked forward to their first showdown as pros.

Fourth-quarter mistakes by Magic hurt the Lakers in game two and game four losses. The series reached a deciding seventh game at the Boston Garden. In that contest, Johnson made only 5 of 14 shots from the field. Near the end of the game, he lost the ball twice. The Celtics won the championship.

*Magic steals a basket from the Celtics' Kevin McHale.*

Magic had never felt so low at the end of a season. His mother called to see how he was doing. "Momma, I just can't talk about it," he told her. His will to win, he believed, was his greatest strength as a player. But it also meant that losses such as this were hard to take.

Led by Larry Bird, the Celtics had set the standard for basketball excellence. To exceed that standard, he would have to work even harder than he had in the past. He knew that winning another championship would make the hurt go away.

And he also knew that Boston would do everything possible to defend its title.

# Chapter 5

# ATHLETE OF THE DECADE

The questions about each other seemed to never end.

"What do you think of Magic's latest pass?" a reporter might ask Larry Bird. And another might question Magic: "Bird was the regular season MVP — when will you win that award?"

Constantly labeled rivals, they grew to think of themselves as enemies. They didn't even shake hands before games.

Then in the summer of 1984, Converse asked them to do a shoe commercial together. They met at Bird's home in French Lick, Indiana. The more they talked, the more they began to like each other. Soon they were riding three-wheelers and laughing together.

Their friendship grew, but the intense rivalry continued. In 1985 the Lakers and Celtics met again for the NBA championship. This time Los Angeles defeated Boston in six games.

Then in 1987, the teams met for the third time in four years. In the decade of the 1980s, each team owned three NBA titles. In head-to-head clashes, each team had one title.

*A smiling Magic picks up his second MVP Award.*

Once again Magic and Bird were in the spotlight.

Los Angeles won two of the first three games. Then, in a thrilling game four, the Lakers clung to a 104–103 lead. With 12 seconds remaining, Bird hit an outside shot to put Boston on top. But with only two seconds left, Magic swished a hook shot to give Los Angeles the victory. The Lakers went on to win the series in six games.

It had been Magic's best year. He won his first regular season MVP award by averaging a career-high 23.9 points per game. He also averaged a league-leading 12.2 assists. He earned his third play-off MVP award for his outstanding performance against Boston.

Johnson's Lakers added yet another championship in 1988, beating Isiah Thomas and the Detroit Pistons in the finals.

In 1989 Magic won his second regular season MVP award. That honor usually goes to high-scoring forwards or centers rather than to play-making guards. Before Johnson, only two guards had received the award (Bob Cousy in 1957 and Oscar Robertson in 1964).

Late in 1989, *Sport* magazine considered several sports

superstars for its Athlete of the Decade award. Football quarterback Joe Montana, tennis great Martina Navratilova, and hockey legend Wayne Gretzky were strong candidates. And, of course, there were basketball's Larry Bird and Magic Johnson.

"The debate will probably always rage over who was 'better' between Bird and Magic," *Sport* wrote. "Let it. What matters is that neither of their styles emphasized stats or records—their games are about winning."

And no one in any sport led his team to more champion- ships during the 1980s than Magic Johnson. In ten years, the Lakers reached the NBA finals eight times and won the title five times. "That's winning," *Sport* stated as the magazine selected Magic Johnson the Athlete of the Decade.

Johnson opened the 1990s with a third regular season MVP award. Then, in 1991 he guided Los Angeles to another NBA championship series. There the Lakers fell to Michael Jordan and the Chicago Bulls.

The talented Jordan was the fastest-rising superstar in the NBA, but no one was more respected than Magic Johnson. Veteran coaches and players knew Magic's flair for the game

*The Athlete of the Decade wins his third MVP Award.*

had started the NBA's surge in success. Since he had entered the league, the average attendance at a pro game had gone from about 10,800 to 15,700. The average player salary was more than six times higher.

When Johnson began a yearly charity basketball game, he was able to bring together many of the league's top players. Between 1986 and 1991, his "Midsummer Night's Magic" in Los Angeles raised $6.5 million for the United Negro College Fund.

Johnson's business interests also grew. "A lot of athletes

just look at the small picture," he said in *Esquire* magazine. "They just want to make the quick-hit, short-term deal." Magic, though, constantly looked toward the future. His many ventures included his own T-shirt company and his own Nintendo game. He also purchased a Pepsi-Cola business in Washington, D.C., with *Black Enterprise* publisher Earl G. Graves as his partner.

Johnson formed another partnership on September 14, 1991, when he married his long-time girlfriend, Earletha "Cookie" Kelly. They had dated on and off since they'd met in 1977 at Michigan State. She earned her degree there in retail, clothing, and textiles, and she later managed a department store in Toledo, Ohio.

About 300 guests attended the wedding in Lansing's Union Missionary Baptist Church. One of Johnson's high-school teammates was his best man, and Isiah Thomas was a grooms-man. The *Detroit News* reported that 3,000 of Magic's fans gathered outside the church.

In late September, Johnson began a Laker exhibition tour that included a trip to Paris. Magic's name, of course, was known worldwide. Several months earlier, a Spanish company

*Magic and Cookie at their wedding*

had asked him to visit Spain. In one day, he drew 17,000 Spaniards to two basketball clinics. Now in Paris, excited crowds chanted, "Magic! Magic!"

On October 25, Johnson was in Salt Lake City with the Lakers when his doctor called and asked to see him. Magic flew back to Los Angeles. There Dr. Mellman told him he had the virus that can lead to AIDS. It had been discovered during a medical exam for an insurance policy. For the next

*Magic poses at the Eiffel Tower while in Paris.*

two weeks, while the tests were double-checked, the public was told he had the flu.

Shortly before announcing the results at the November 7 news conference, Magic called several close friends to tell them. At first Isiah refused to believe it. Pat Riley, Magic's former coach, listened quietly, too stunned to talk. Larry Bird cried.

From the time Magic announced that he carried the AIDS virus, many admired the way he talked about his future goals. Someday, he said, he wanted to own an NBA team. Magic's comments didn't surprise those who knew him well. He had always tried to look toward the future.

Long before, while he was growing up in Lansing, that had been true. Scheduled to meet his friends at the playground for a basketball game, he often arrived early. Then, before the others came, he ran wind sprints. He knew the hard work would help him during the fourth quarter of a future game.

And he had displayed his foresight during his business career. Sitting in a meeting in a suit and tie, he always considered the long-term outlook for each business deal. Because of his careful planning, by 1991 he was making at least $9 million from his interests outside pro basketball. That was three times

*Magic speaks with President Bush after joing the National Commission on AIDS.*

his salary as a Laker player.

During his life, Magic has learned that, each day, everyone makes decisions that affect their future — whether for good or bad.

Today, in basketball camps and in schools, he talks to young people about some of those choices. He answers questions about his achievements in basketball and business, and he openly discusses mistakes he's made because of his sexual life-style. The courage he has shown while trying to help others will long be remembered.

In fact, fans have not wanted to forget Magic. They voted him to the starting lineup for the 1992 All-Star game, and the fans were not disappointed. He scored 25 points in the contest and was named MVP. The next week, during a halftime

*Magic shows he hasn't lost his touch in the 1992 All-Star game.*

*Former teammate Kareem Abdul-Jabbar talks with his friend at the ceremony retiring Magic's Lakers uniform.*

ceremony at the Forum, Johnson's uniform was retired. No other Laker will ever wear number 32.

For most basketball fans, though, the clearest images of Magic will always be of him in his Laker uniform. They'll recall Magic, the dynamic rookie, leading the 1980 upset of the 76ers. And they'll never forget Magic, at the peak of his career, sinking the hook shot that beat the Celtics in 1987. And they'll remember Magic, the classy veteran, breaking the career assist record in 1991 and crediting his parents and teammates.

A happy moment for Magic and his wife came on June 4, 1992, when their son, Earvin Johnson III, was born. Doctors reported that neither Cookie nor the baby was infected with HIV.

So many special moments, all brightened in memory by that magical smile.

# EARVIN "MAGIC" JOHNSON'S BASKETBALL STATISTICS

## For Michigan State University

| Year | G | Pts | FG% | FT% | Reb | Asst |
|------|------|------|------|------|------|------|
| 1977-78 | 30 | 17.0 | .458 | .785 | 7.9 | 7.4 |
| 1978-79 | 32 | 17.1 | .468 | .842 | 7.3 | 8.4 |
| Totals | 62 | 17.1 | .463 | .816 | 7.6 | 7.9 |

## For Los Angeles Lakers

| Year | G | Pts | FG% | FT% | Reb | Asst |
|------|------|------|------|------|------|------|
| 1979-80 | 77 | 18.0 | .530 | .810 | 7.7 | 7.3 |
| 1980-81 | 37 | 21.6 | .532 | .760 | 8.6 | 8.6 |
| 1981-82 | 78 | 18.6 | .537 | .760 | 9.6 | 9.5 |
| 1982-83 | 79 | 16.8 | .548 | .800 | 8.6 | 10.5 |
| 1983-84 | 67 | 17.6 | .565 | .810 | 7.3 | 13.1 |
| 1984-85 | 77 | 18.3 | .561 | .843 | 6.2 | 12.6 |
| 1985-86 | 72 | 18.8 | .526 | .871 | 5.9 | 12.6 |
| 1986-87 | 80 | 23.9 | .522 | .848 | 6.3 | 12.2 |
| 1987-88 | 72 | 19.6 | .492 | .853 | 6.2 | 11.9 |
| 1988-89 | 77 | 22.5 | .509 | .911 | 7.9 | 12.8 |
| 1989-90 | 79 | 22.3 | .480 | .890 | 6.6 | 11.5 |
| 1990-91 | 79 | 19.4 | .477 | .906 | 7.0 | 12.5 |
| Totals | 874 | 19.7 | .521 | .848 | 7.3 | 11.4* |

*Career assist total of 9,921 is all-time NBA record.

# SELECTED BIBLIOGRAPHY

The *Detroit News*, several articles, 1991.

Johnson, Earvin "Magic," and Roy S. Johnson.
  *Magic's Touch*. Reading, Mass.: Addison-Wesley Publishing
  Company, Inc., 1989.

Johnson, Earvin "Magic," and Richard Levin. *Magic*. New York: The
  Viking Press, 1983.

Keith, Larry. "A Class with Class." *Sports Illustrated*,
  November 27, 1978, 48.

*Lansing State Journal*, several articles, March 27, 1977.

Looney, Douglas S. "And for My Next Trick, I'll ..." *Sports Illustrated*, April 30, 1979, 28.

*Los Angeles Times*, numerous articles, 1979 through 1991.

Lupica, Mike. "Do You Believe in Magic?" *Esquire*, April 1990, 73.

"Magic Passes Robertson for NBA Assist Record." *Jet*, May 6, 1991,
  46.

Newman, Bruce. "Magic Faces the Music." *Sports Illustrated*, May
  13, 1985, 82.

Shah, Diane K. "Double Helping of Magic." *Newsweek*, March 17,
  1980, 59.

"The *Sport* Athlete of the Decade: Magic Johnson." *Sport*, October
  1989, 96.

# INDEX

## ABOUT THE AUTHOR

Rick L. Johnson is the author of two other Taking Part books, *Jim Abbott: Beating the Odds* and *Bo Jackson: Baseball/Football Superstar.* In the research for his most recent book, the author says that interviews with Magic Johnson's grade school coach and his high school coach were especially helpful.

Mr. Johnson also has written articles and short stories for a wide variety of publications. He has won first place for column writing and first place for sports pages in the Kansas Press Association Better Newspaper Contest. A graduate of the University of Kansas School of Journalism, he and his wife, Diane, live in Concordia, Kansas.